DESERT
IGUANAS

by Judith Jango-Cohen

Lerner Publications Company • Minneapolis

The publisher wishes to thank Dr. Bradford Hollingsworth from the Department of Herpetology at the San Diego Natural History Museum for his help with the preparation of this book.

This book is available in two editions:
Library binding by Lerner Publications Company, a division of Lerner Publishing Group
Soft cover by First Avenue Editions, an imprint of Lerner Publishing Group
241 First Avenue North
Minneapolis, MN 55401 U.S.A.

Website address: www.lernerbooks.com

Words in *italic type* are explained in a glossary on page 30.

Library of Congress Cataloging-in-Publication Data

Jango-Cohen, Judith.
    Desert iguanas / by Judith Jango-Cohen.
        p.   cm. — (Pull ahead books)
    Includes index.
    HC ISBN 0-8225-3635-8 (lib. bdg. : alk. paper)
    SC ISBN 0-8225-3642-0 (pbk. : alk paper)
    1. Desert iguana—Juvenile literature. [1. Desert
iguana. 2. Iguanas] I. Title. II. Series.
QL666.L25 J36 2001
597.95'421754—dc21   00-009317

Manufactured in the United States of America
1 2 3 4 5 6 – JR – 06 05 04 03 02 01

Look at those claws
and that bumpy skin!

Is this a dinosaur?

No! This animal is an iguana.
Iguanas are *reptiles*.

Reptiles have scaly skin.
Scales are hard like your nails.

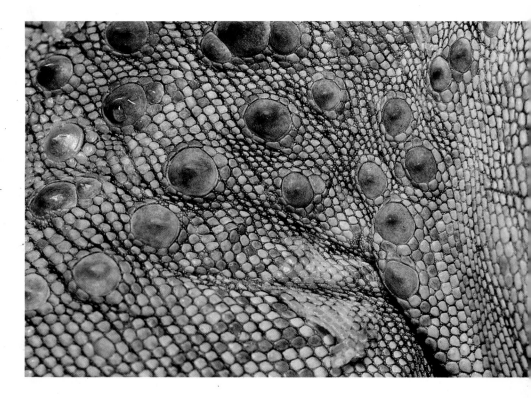

Hard scales protect reptiles.
They also hold in water.

With scaly skin, reptiles can live in dry places.

They can live in hot places, too. Where do iguanas live?

These iguanas live near the sea.

Other iguanas live in rain forests.

Desert iguanas live
in the hot and dry desert.

Most desert animals rest
in the shade in the hot afternoon.

What do desert iguanas do?

Desert iguanas *bask* in the sun
in the hot afternoon.

Iguanas bask to stay warm.
Iguanas are *ectotherms*.

Ectotherms cannot make
their own body heat.

Their body heat changes to match
the warmth or cold around them.

Even a desert iguana
can get too hot.

Then it climbs into a shady bush
to cool off.

The iguana uses its claws to climb.

The claws of an iguana are sharp.
They grip the bark.

An iguana finds food in the bushes.

Desert iguanas eat
leaves, fruits, and flowers.

An iguana eats and basks
in its *territory*.

A territory is an iguana's
very own place.

An iguana keeps other iguanas
out of its territory.

A desert iguana can be hard to see in its territory.

The iguana's skin blends in with the stones, sand, and trees.

Animals that blend in with their background are *camouflaged*.

Can you find the camouflaged iguana hiding here?

19

A camouflaged iguana can hide from *predators*.

Predators are animals that hunt and eat other animals.

An iguana can fight predators with its claws.

It can also flick its tail like a whip.

An iguana may run
if it does not want to fight.

But what if a predator grabs
the iguana by the tail?

Snap! Its tail drops off, and the iguana keeps running.

Soon a new tail may grow back.

The iguana runs into its *burrow* to hide.

A burrow is a hole that the iguana digs in the sand.

Desert iguanas lay their eggs in burrows.

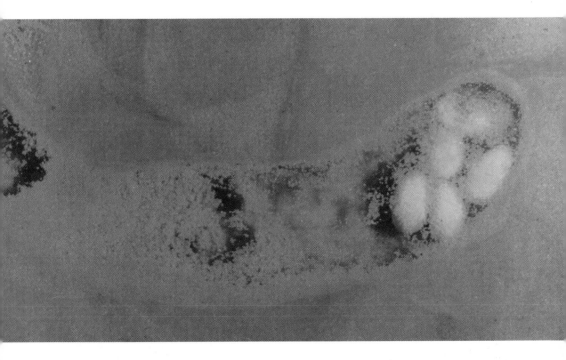

Then one day, the eggs hatch.
What do baby iguanas look like?

Baby iguanas have long tails, scales, and sharp claws.

They look like little
dinosaurs!

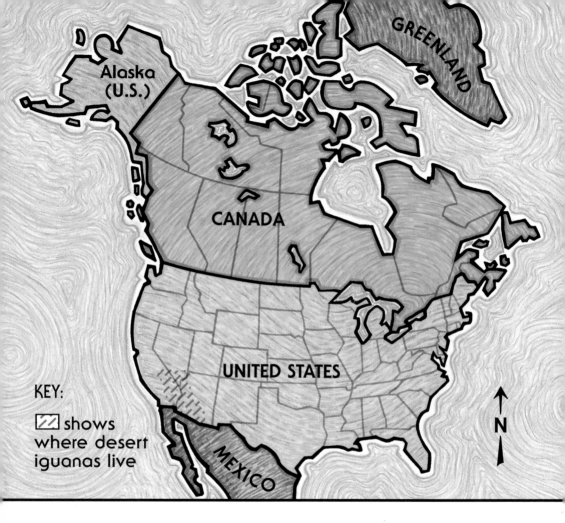

KEY:

▨ shows where desert iguanas live

Alaska (U.S.)

GREENLAND

CANADA

UNITED STATES

MEXICO

N

Find your state or province on this map.
Do desert iguanas live near you?

Parts of a Desert Iguana's Body

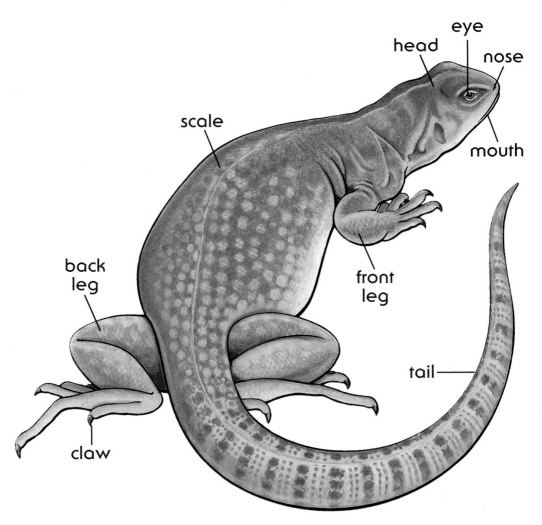

eye

head

nose

scale

mouth

back
leg

front
leg

tail

claw

Glossary

bask: to lie in the sun to warm the body. Iguanas must bask to stay alive.

burrow: a hole that an iguana digs in the ground. Iguanas hide and lay their eggs in burrows.

camouflage: coloring or covering that helps an animal blend in with its surroundings

ectotherms: animals whose body heat changes to match the warmth or cold around them

predators: animals that hunt and eat other animals

reptiles: crawling or creeping animals that have backbones. Most reptiles have scaly skins and lay eggs.

scales: flat, hard plates on an iguana's skin. Scales protect a reptile's body and hold in water.

territory: an animal's very own place. An iguana keeps other iguanas out of its territory.

Hunt and Find

- **basking** iguanas on pages 9–11
- an iguana in its **burrow** on page 24
- **camouflaged** iguanas on pages 18–19
- iguanas **climbing** on pages 12–14, 21
- iguanas **eating** on pages 15–16
- iguana **scales** on pages 3, 5–6

The publisher wishes to extend special thanks to our **series consultant,** Sharyn Fenwick. An elementary math-science specialist, Mrs. Fenwick was the recipient of the National Science Teachers Association 1991 Distinguished Teaching Award. In 1992, representing the state of Minnesota at the elementary level, she received the Presidential Award for Excellence in Math and Science Teaching.

About the Author

Eliot Cohen

Judith Jango-Cohen grew up in a Boston apartment with cats, turtles, and tropical fish. She loved learning about plants and animals and earned a degree in biology. For ten years she taught science to children. When her own children were born, she began working at her home in Burlington, Massachusetts, as a writer. With her husband, Eliot, and her children, Jennifer and Steven, Judith often visits the desert. When she looks carefully, she finds treasures in the sand—like desert iguanas!

Photo Acknowledgments

The photographs in this book are reproduced through courtesy of: **Visuals Unlimited:** (© S. Strickland/Naturescapes) front cover, (© Ken Lucas) p. 18, (© Joe McDonald) pp. 19, 24, (© Maslowski) p. 20, (© John Gerlach) p. 22; **Photo Researchers:** (© Dan Suzio) back cover, pp. 12, 13, 14, 21, 31, (© E. R. Degginger) p. 8, (© Tom McHugh) p. 23; **Tom Stack & Associates:** (© Thomas Kitchin) pp. 3, 4, 5, (© Joe McDonald) pp. 6, 7; © Joe McDonald/McDonald Wildlife Photography, p. 9; **Bruce Coleman, Inc.:** (© M. P. L. Fogden) p. 10, (© Joe McDonald) p. 11, (© Jeff Foott) p. 15, (© Tom Brakefield) p. 16, (© John H. Hoffman) p. 17; © Dr. Allan Muth, Boyd Deep Canyon Desert Research Center, p. 25; © Bradford D. Hollingsworth, Department of Herpetology, San Diego Natural History Museum, pp. 26–27.